Pep Talk Poetry

a tiny book of pep talks to remind you
that you're an unmitigated badass.

emily haines lloyd

DEDICATION

For little girls who grow up in trailer parks
and grow into heroes.

CONTENTS

ACKNOWLEDGMENTS

For my sister who is the inspiration.

For my husband who is the foundation.

For our children who are the incarnation.

For my friends who are the inebriation.

INTRODUCTION

I am an optimist. At least when it comes to other people's lives. I love being a cheerleader and a confidant and a fire under the ass of a friend who needs it.

However, I have not always taken my own advice or accepted the kind and encouraging words of strangers. That's when I started an Instagram feed called *Buddha-ish*.

It was meant to be a series of pep talks to anyone who needed one, but mostly – for me.

While I love social media for many different reasons, the words and images can hit you in a moment and be gone just seconds later. I wanted to make sure that for those who needed it – there was a constant reminder that each of us is an unmitigated badass.

And so, you hold in your hands a little book of my best pep talks for you and me. Gobble them up all at once, take them one day at a time, or close your eyes and flip to any page. Guaranteed there's a little glimmer of something to make your day better. Well, not actually guaranteed, because you bought this book. Sorry, you're stuck with it.

But mostly, I want to remind us all that we are worthy of encouragement, joy, and love. That's what you're holding in your hands – my heart on my sleeve, my hand on your shoulder. Now, take these words and get on with your bad self.

EMILY HAINES LLOYD

BELIEVE

EMILY HAINES LLOYD

BEAUTIFUL MESS

hey, you!
yeah, you.

the one with the wild eyes
and devilish smile,

the one with dreams
still bouncing around
in your busy mind –

i like you – a lot.

LIVE WILD

rawr,
you magnificent beast.

OPEN DOORS

the door is open.

all you have to do
is muster every ounce
of courage you have
and then –

walk through it.

STILL HERE

you're here,
against all odds.

has anyone told you
you're a singular soul
with a
shitload of pluck?

well, you are.

which probably has a
little something to do
with your present location.

BE BRAVE

the world
can be big
and scary.

but your courage
is even
bigger.

and while it's not technically "scarier,"
it certainly does know
how to handle itself.

TAP THAT

tap into
your greatness.

you were born
into matchless splendor.

you have no choice
but to deliver
on your divine
birthright.

SIT UP & SHINE

back straight.
release your shoulders.
chin out.
deep breath.

(breathes)

now,
let the glowing commence.

STRONGER

if thor
and the hulk
had a baby –

it would be almost,
but not nearly,
as fierce
as you.

THRILLER

be thrilled by the notion
of your own life.

find suspense
and intrigue
and possibly even
an unexpected twist or two.

no one has ever heard
your story.
It has not even been
fully written.

you are the surprise ending
that no one saw coming.

FULL PACKAGE

you're already the
full package,
the real deal.

you've got "it"
and so much more.

now it's time
to act like it.

BELIEVE

believe the hype,
the hoopla,
the whispers
of your wonderfulness.

it's all true,
you know.

you're amazeballs.

best go ahead
and get used to it.

YOU ARE TOTALLY, FUCKING MAGNIFICENT

oh my gosh! did you forget?
even for a minute?

you don't need perfectly-applied lipstick to be
magnificent.
the kids don't need matching socks for you to be
magnificent.
dinner doesn't have to be hot for you to be
magnificent.
the workout doesn't need to be crushed for you to be
magnificent.
the art doesn't need to be flawless,
the laundry can wait,
there will be another meeting tomorrow
and another one the day after that.

the only thing you need to be in order to be
magnificent – is yourself.

remember that –
there'll be a test tomorrow.

YOU ARE MAGIC

in case you forgot
for one glorious
goddamn second.

BELIEVE IT

you are
a wonder.

seriously.

believe it.

WHIPSHIT

you are
the whippitiest whip
that ever
whipped.

APPLAUSE

can you hear that?

that tiny bit of noise,
almost a ringing
in your ears?

that is every
ecstatic molecule
of the universe
clapping wildly
just for you.

don't try
to remember
what you did to deserve
the standing ovation
of creation.

you were deserving
before you even took
your first breath.

all you have to do
is feel
the joy
at the center of your chest
and
take your bow.

YOU ROCK

like mosh pit,
head-banging
rock.

so, get on with your bad self.

ORDINARY

you make ordinary
look extraordinary.

just sayin'.

WHY ME?

why you,
indeed.

because
there was something
to learn,
something
to feel.

there was something
you longed for,
something
unseen.

there was something
forbidden
you needed to try,
something
that scared you
or a tear to be cried.

why you?

because there was
no one else
who could
pick up the pieces
and put them together
in a way
so new and inspiring,

that the world
would have been
empty without it.

why you?

because it was your
destiny
to try new things
and
blow us all away.

TRUST

there is a voice
that says –

"you can't do it.
you're not strong enough."

that is not your voice.

that is the voice of
fear
and fear
never believed in
itself.

instead –
listen to the voice
that quivers
as it whispers –

"you are an unmitigated badass
and you were born
to do hard things."

trust that voice.
that voice knows
what the fuck it's talking about.

LEGENDARY

there is nothing
in this world,
that if you put your whole heart into,
isn't the stuff of legends.

because legends
give it all,
fall down,
and give again.

you're legendary, my friend.

BLOCKADE

there is nothing
that could possibly
stand between
you and your wildest dreams –

except the tiniest shred
of self-doubt.

it's one hell of
a speed bump,
but if you see it coming,
slow down,
and keep moving forward
instead of turning around –

you'll be just fine.

DISCOVERY

the only person
you have an obligation to
is yourself.

and the only way
you could ever
fail yourself
is to stop
discovering
your own
true and perfect
beauty.

SHINE ON

twinkle, twinkle
my little
badass
star.

THE WAY

the way
you shine,
and sparkle,
and glow
is just another example
of how you brighten
the world.

so,
thanks.

IMAGINE

imagine,
if you will,
a life filled with
joy,
adventure,
comfort,
and peace.

then take one
giant step back
and watch
as each and every dream
you imagined
comes flying at you
like a meteor shower.

BEAUTY MARK

if "X" really did
mark the spot,
there would be two
large lines
crossing one another
right over you.

because you are
the spot.

you are the place
where beauty,
and kindness,
and badassery
come together –
creating the most
amazing treasure
the world will ever know.

THE ONE

you are the one
you've been waiting for.

and you were
one thousand percent
worth the wait.

NO LIMITS

there is nothing
you can't do
with some
belief in yourself,
a little stamina,
a dash of pluck,
and a roll of duct tape.

you've got this.

WORTHY

your worthiness
is not pending
anyone's approval.

you were born worthy,
born ready,
and born deserving
of every good thing the world
has to offer –

including your
own love and
affection.

(mic drop)

THE LEGEND

it's already true –
that you are a legend
of your own making.

you are the hero
you've longed and waited for.

you are the wo/man,
the myth,
the legend.

so,
start acting like it.

THE SECRET

what if you were told
that all the things
you ever dreamed of
were within your power
to have?

well,
you're being told now.

so, get to it already.

RECEIVE

you're ready,
right now,
to gracefully,
purposefully,
and wholly receive
the life
of your dreams.

DREAMY

all you ever
dared to dream
is a fraction
of what
you are capable
of manifesting.

you are a badass.

get used to it.

PEP TALK POETRY

EMILY HAINES LLOYD

LET

GO

SURRENDER IS BEAUTIFUL

you are too tender
too sweet
too fragile
too kind
to hold on to things
that weigh you down.

you deserve to float
and fly.

so clip the string,
cut the chain,
put down the burdens

and let that shit go.

OH, HONEY. RELAX

time is not for cramming in
activity.
time is for living
fluidly.

you don't have to DO anything.
you must only be.

and if you cannot do that
then, please, for your own sake –
take one deep,
soothing breath and
unclench ever so slightly.

VULNERABILITY IS BADASS

make your heart soft.

put down your guard and
lower your shield.

muster the strength
to see
and to feel.

steep in it
until it breaks
you open.

make your heart soft.

only then will you know
just how strong you are.

FOR FUCK'S SAKE – BREATHE

do not gasp for air.

it will come
as easily as a blink.
it will save you
as completely as forgiveness.

take one deep breath to
change your day.

take one more to
change the world.

SAVE IT

save your sorry
and
you'll save
your soul.

SO CHILL

some days a smooth,
mellow vibe
washes over
and
you are saved
from fears and
old wounds.

you are reminded
of the breath
and the source
and your good strong bones
and muscle and blood –
all the things that
hold you to your body.

so, take another deep breath
to connect your body
to your brain
and your brain to your soul
and your soul to your purpose –
which is as simple as
being yourself.

then, let the smooth,
mellow vibe
wash over you
and
be saved.

SURVIVAL KIT

today,
if you are looking for
a life boat,
something to keep you afloat
as you feel
the water rising –

say these words…

"you are forgiven."

say them aloud,
say them often,
say them to yourself.

whatever you may have done,
what actions you may have taken,
what paths you chose,
what advise you ignored,
what promises you broke,
what words said in fear,
what lies told to yourself or others –

forgive yourself.

forgive yourself often.
forgive yourself sincerely.
forgive yourself with all the love you can muster.

and mean it.

NOPE. JUST NOPE.

there are so many little piles
of crap
trying to jack up your day.

don't let 'em.

put those wonder woman wristbands
to work
and
pay no mind
to ridiculous shit.

BAGGAGE CLAIM

watch the luggage carousel
go 'round and 'round
and simply refuse
to pick up
any baggage
that holds vestiges of a life
you no longer want.

DEAR STRESS

put it down.

you cannot stand when yoked
with the weight of the world.

you cannot fly
with your gaze downward.

kick stress to the curb

and make sure to
double-bag that shit.

BAMBOOZLED

at your core
you know who you are
and what you're about.

don't let another person
or set of circumstances
trip you up
or keep you down.

do not let fear bamboozle you.

CHEER UP

cheer up when you're
goddamn good and ready.

give yourself a freaking
moment of grief
if you need it.

don't worry,
your superhero cape
will be waiting
for you.

promise.

CRAY-CRAY

if you're spinning
a bit too wild
and
you're holding on
by the seat of your pants –

take a deep breath
and watch
how sinking slowly
into yourself
will soothe your nerves
and
calm your cray.

HAPPINESS PROJECT

some days
there is nothing
to do
but
curl up the corners
of your mouth
and enjoy
the ride.

WAIT

everything
and
everyone
in the world
that floats
with ease
and
grace,

learned
to do so
by
chilling
the eff out
and
learning
patience.

GROW

EMILY HAINES LLOYD

ENLIGHTENMENT AIN'T EASY

struggle,
strain,
and push against the quiet
where feelings are the loudest sound of all.
then remember to keep going,
'cause enlightenment ain't easy.

FIRST THE GESTURE. THEN THE GRACE.

when the universe asks you to dance
say "yes."

prepare to step on its toes,
as you keep trying to lead
both backwards and in heels.

the universe reminds you
not to listen outward,
but inward.

that's where the real music plays.

then the steps come easy –
the beat is as steady as
your own heart.

the universe steps and you counter –
like fred and ginger.

together you are magic.

FALLING DOWN IS BEAUTIFUL

a skinned knee
is like an abstract
painting.

you may never fully
understand it.

you may only
remember
how you felt at the sight of the
agonizing beauty.

we tend not to remember
how we rose after,
how we limped
until we could walk,
how we tended to our pain
and learned
from it.

the fall is only
where we begin.

the rising
is the rest
of the jaw-dropping story.

BIG THINGS

you are only human,

but that
is no small thing.

you are made of
fucking stardust.

you are made of
the same stuff
as mountains
and glaciers
and beluga whales
and champagne.

you are only human –
true.

but you can do
big things.

LEAN IN

there is so much
that is
weird and
wonderful
in this world.

it is not
meticulously curated,
or airbrushed,
or edited.

it is messy,
and real,
and unable to be recreated
or mass produced.

so keep your eyes
and ears poised
to pick up
those tiny glimmers of
weirdness and
wonderfulness –

and then
lean into the magic.

SHINE

you can't help but sparkle
and shine.

you are made from stars.

you are a billion tiny particles
that once reflected
the absolute
power of the universe.

your birth was miraculous.
your life
is too.

so, when faced with
the impossible
remember who the fuck you are.

you are stardust from the heavens.

shine – little star.
shine.

NOW IS THE TIME

don't wait.

there is not nearly enough time
for all the possibility
stored up inside you.

do it now.
say it now.

don't hesitate.
don't pause.
don't talk yourself out of it.

the time is now
and
you were built for this.

WAKE UP

oh, lovely –
it's time to flutter open
those beautiful eyes
and take in all the world
has to offer.

get after it!

(don't forget to brush your teeth
and slap on some
deodorant.)

but mostly,
just try to smile
and
enjoy the exquisite ride.

BE THE SPARK

when it is time to act,
it is time.

like, now.
like, post haste.

like, no permission slip needed to do
that which you know in your heart
must be done.

OM

it is the sound of
whitman's barbaric yawp

of wallace's cry
for freedom

of king's letter from
a birmingham jail

of anthony's call for
suffrage for her sisters

of mandela's
long walk to freedom

of rilke's letter
to a young poet

of davis' vow
to change the things she cannot accept

of obama's rally
to go high when they go low

and obama's audacity
of hope

the om is sacred,
unique,
and undeniable.

what is your om?

ONLY YOU

only you know your own heart.

so,
listen closely
and
follow where it leads.

NOT AN OPTION

you cannot fail.

you can only fuck things up
a little.

NOW NOW NOW

what is keeping you
from doing
that which your heart
is begging you
to do?

now tell that thing ·
to go
fuck off.

SUMMON YOURSELF

call forth your
indominable soul
like the freaking formidable kraken
that it is.

LIFE LESSONS

in each loss
there is a lesson.

so, we must learn
to warmly greet and honor
each fuck up
and every train wreck.

SORRY NOT SORRY

there is no shame
in your game.

live
life
unapologetically.

HAPPY HAPPY. JOY JOY

your business is joy.

now, go
and
earn your paycheck.

BEAUTIFUL FIRE

is there anything
more beautiful –

than your soul when
it's set
aflame?

CONSPIRE

you are a co-conspirator
with the
universe.

it's time to get together
and hatch
the most beautiful freaking plan
for your life.

HONOR YOUR DREAMS

so much heart
and soul
went into them –
it's the least you can do.

IMAGINE

you owe it
to yourself
to imagine better.

then stand back
and be amazed
at what happens next.

A PIRATE'S LIFE

it's time to hoist
your own sail
and
point your ship
in a direction
that sets your soul on fire.

DO IT

"do what?"
you ask?

everything you ever
had the good sense
and audacity to dream.

plus a few things
you haven't even thought of –

yet.

YOU CAN

you can do
so much more
than your confidence
thinks you can.

so let's put
confidence in a time out
and let bravery
explore the ol' sandbox
for a bit.

so. much. better.

LIVE LARGE

too many of us
have played too small
for too long.

playing small
doesn't serve one's soul.

and we are in the fucking soul business.

MOON-STYLE

between you
and me
and the moon –
darkness
doesn't stand a chance.

maybe you don't feel
like you can shine
on your own
right now.

just keep an eye out
for the beautiful glow
of others
or the things
that inspire and move you –

and
reflect that light back
to the world.

GPS

do you spend too much time
doing and becoming,
and not enough time
feeling and letting go?

it's time
to take the ol' heart
out for a spin.
kick the tires
and fill up the tank.

it's time to hit the road
and trust your gut
will take you exactly
where you're meant
to go.

your gut has GPS –
trust that shit.

DREAMER

your dream is not
silly.

it is not frivolous
or
even impossible.

it is the seed of hope
that you are entrusted
to water,
feed,
and nurture
until it grows
strong and tall.

it is the gift to the world
that only you
can give.

BE THE CHANGE

don't change
to fit into
someone else's
corrugated, pre-fab
box.

you are too magnificently
and gloriously
unique for that.

you are bespoke.

your edges,
your curves,
your vibration,
your glow –

it will never look exactly the same
in your lifetime or any other.

and while you're sitting there
in your one-of-a-kindness,
try to remember
that everyone else
is equally magnificent
and glorious
in their own uniqueness.

they too are a one-of-a-kind miracle,
they too deserve to be cherished
and not changed.

so, when you find yourself
unhappy with your
circumstance –
the only change
you have the right to make,
is to yourself.

just don't be surprised
if your little adjustments
and wiggles
inspire those around you
to see your shine
and reflect the same.

BE YOU

because there is nothing else,
in this great, big, beautiful world
that you could
possibly
be.

DREAM WORK

your dream
is not too big.

it is not too
complicated
or
unattainable.

your dream
is worth the time
and effort
you put into it.

but never forget –

your worth is not
tied up in your dream.

your dream
and the hope of it
coming true
will never be more
important or
satisfying
than realizing
that you,
the dreamer,
are the real miracle.

THIS TIME

this little bit
of time and space
belongs to you
and
no one else.

it is your canvas,
your clean slate,
your piece
of history.

the only question is –
how fully
will you share yourself
with the world?

HARD CHOICES

the decision
was always yours
to make.

it was the simple,
but life-altering,
choice
to be your own
authentic self

or a designer-imposter
version
of something you once admired.

the choice was simple,
but the choosing was hard.

guess what?

it's never too late
to choose
yourself.

DIFFERENCE

out there,
in the distance,
where injustice breaks our hearts
and
the insurmountable appears
on the horizon –

is a place and a moment
that exists just for you
to make a difference.

just little ol' you
and your great big
powerful
heart.

SHINE ON

shine
with so much brilliance
that others
think you are a star,
dazzling the galaxy
by just being.

bring that twinkle
to each
and every day.

watch,
one day,
they'll name
an entire universe after you.

UNDISCOVERED

do not wait for someone
to come along
and unearth
all the treasures
of your soul.

you already have
your own pick axe,
shovel,
and wheelbarrow –

now, go inward,
reveal who you really are,
along with all your
undiscovered riches.

ENVY

live your life
with so much
guts and gumption
that everyone
will simply turn green
with envy.

ALL IN

are you really, truly
"all in"
on this beautiful life
you've been given?

not halfway,
not one toe in –
but all in?

give it some thought
and then
cannonball
right into the deep end.

WEIRD ONE

be the wild one,
the anything-but-average one.

be the one
that encourages others
to buck the system
and
ignore lines in the sand.

be the one
that laughs at normal
and
strives for weirdness.

WAITING

what are you
waiting for?

permission?
granted.

the right time?
now.

courage?
swimming in it.

support?
your own two legs.

time really is
flying,
so let's get to it,
shall we?

LET'S GO

time doesn't always wait
for you to be ready.

so, let's hit
the road,
start the
journey,
take the chance,
risk the fall,
be the hero
of your own story.

you only have to be as ready
as the first step.

THE KEY

there is only
one lock
worth taking a
bent bobby pin to
and jiggling it about
to try and bust
the lock open.

it's the one that is
holding your heart
against its will,
as it tries desperately
to be that which it was born
to be.

NEW AGE ARCHEOLOGY

dig, dig, dig.

dig deeper.

keep digging.

dig and dig
and dig
some more.

dig until you find
the one-of-a-kind,
otherworldly,
uniquely divine
truth –
that is you.

NEW WAY

there are so many ways
to think different,
to dream bigger,
to breathe deeper,
to laugh harder.

so find the way
that is profoundly
and uniquely
yours.

EMILY HAINES LLOYD

LOVE

EMILY HAINES LLOYD

HEART (aka Be Kind to Yo'self)

oh heart,
you did so good today.

you beat in time
and pumped the blood
and fed the cells
and allowed the blood to flow
and find its way back home.

you are a miracle in this body –
even if we forget to say "thanks"
every now and then.

you are the center,
the core,
and a constant friend.

you make things work
when nothing else does.

you bind us to this world
where we're grateful to be
and so
we are grateful to you.

thank you, friend.
thank you from the bottom of our...

YOU ARE LOVED

the universe told me
to tell you
that it has
the most ridiculous
crush on you.

PRIORITIES

love you first.

the end.

LOVE IT ALL

the messy
the frantic
the foolish
the manic

the joyful
the bliss
the better
than this

the simple
the sage
the impish
the rage

the sweetness
the sour
the moment
the hour

the effort
the prize
the time
when it flies

the freshness
the foul
the laughter
the growl

the hustle
the test
and then finally
the rest.

B.A.

how does it feel
knowing that you are,
in the very core
of your being,
a total badass?

pretty good, right?

CHOOSE YOU

be your own
greatest
admirer.

YOU BELONG

don't ever
get over
the idea
that you, and me,
and she,
and them –
all of us
are made of the same bits
of universal matter.

so you could never,
not ever,
be alone
in this world.

you belong
to us.

TRAPEZE

we're all flying
through the air
with anything
but the greatest
of ease.

don't worry,
we're your net
and
you'll get the hang of it.

and if not –
we'll keep
catching you.

ONE REASON

there's only one reason
to put down
your guard,
open your heart,
and pour
your love
into someone else –

and that is
absolutely
no reason
at all.

A LOVE STORY

love this one, crazy
and ridiculous life
you've been given.

imperfections and all.

ANOTHER LOVE STORY

there once was a soul.

and there once was another soul.

each of them loved
themselves
with such
glorious kindness
and spoke only
tender words to themselves.

then that soul
and that other soul

went out into the world,
never meeting one another,
and lived happily ever after.

because they were
perfectly in love
with their own self.

the end.

YET ANOTHER LOVE STORY

the whole universe
exists
to bask us in love,
so that we can do the same
for those
who surround us.

YOU ARE LOVED

by me,
by them,
by us.

who are –
me, them, and us?

don't worry about
that just now.

just know
we are all out here –
waiting for you
to open your heart
and create a space
for us.

SUPER STAR

there is
no award,
no promotion,
no commendation,
no raise,
no deal,
no medal,
no prize,
no jackpot –

that could ever
shine a light
on your true worth,
more than
the trust, love,
and respect
of those closest to you.

it's easy to be a winner,
when you start
close to home.

LOVE, ME

has there ever been
a more gloriously
terrifying
question
than the one
where
you ask
someone to love you?

has there ever been
a more beautifully
generous
answer
than –

sure,
why not?

try it out on yourself.
dare you.

ETC.

PEACE IT TOGETHER

find peace
within.

find joy.
find grace.

find kindness
and
forgiveness.

find love
and
connection.

find patience.
find acceptance.

find peace
within.

SLEEP HEALS

you can grow bones
in your sleep.

think about what some
zzz's could do
to strengthen your soul.

OKAY

oh honey,
it's all gonna
be okay.

first you have to
think it,
then you have to
feel it,
then you can
believe it.

RESILIENCE

your resilience
is radiant.

it reminds us
to hold on.

to grasp for
even a finger hold
and keep
hanging in there.

you are stronger
than you think.
you are more complete
than you believe.

you remember
and learn from the pain.

but don't forget
the fury
that brought you back
from the edge.

you may have been
shattered,

but there is always
a way back
from broken.

PERFECT IS FOR SUCKERS

do not,
under any circumstances,
let perfectionism
put a choke hold
on your joy.

DANCE PARTIES WELCOME

step, touch.
step, touch.

shake your bootie.

step, touch.
step, touch.

wave your hands
in the air.

repeat
with some frequency.

REDEFINING THE BAR

so much pressure
to be perfect.

and timely
and clever
and communicative
and friendly
and thoughtful
and sexy
and emotionally stable
and loving
and helpful
and generous with your time
and mindful of your finances
and coiffed
and ensure your socks are matching
and all the other things.

but today, maybe we're doing our best
and you're doing your best
and the kids are still alive…

…and that's enough.

CREATE A CLEARING

make a little space.

then stand back
and watch the magic
rush in.

UNDONE

it is rarely too late
to walk things back,
to say sorry,
or to un-fuck a thing
that needs un-fucking.

PRICKLY

life can be prickly,
but that doesn't mean
you have to be.

START WITH YOU

need more peace?
need more love?
need more kindness?
need more…more?

there's only one place to start.

STRONG

(strokes hair and touches forehead to yours.)

don't let a broken heart
break you.

FUCK THE UMBRELLA

my dearest,
it's gonna rain –

plenty.

and then plenty more.

but so little is gained by
bracing for it.

IT ALL

the good,
the bad,
and the ugly.

hold it close,
give it a squeeze,
and thank it.

it all has value.

so treasure it,
don't trash it.

'kay?

A PRIMER IN LEADERSHIP

always
always
always

take the first step
in love.

PARTY SHOES

it's time to
break out
the party shoes
and
celebrate every moment
of your perfectly lovely
and ridiculous
life.

PROMISES, PROMISES

of all the promises you'll make,
the ones you break
or keep
to yourself
are the ones that matter most.

CHOOSE ADVENTURE

life is too fleeting
and precious
to be boring.

ON THE BRINK

oh, to live on the brink!

the views, my friends.
the views!

HELL TO THE NO

sometimes we need
reminding –

"no"
is a complete sentence.

SHADE

today,
let's remember to
give shade,
not throw it.

be a great, big canopy
of love
for someone
to sit safely under.

RAVE ON

you are a living,
breathing
glowstick.

your purpose is
to shine.

UNKIND

unkind is uncool.

it's really that simple –
except it's not.

because it means remembering
to include ourselves
on that list.

we're so unkind to ourselves.
all. the. damn. time.

we need to pour as much understanding
and humanity
into our own cup,
until it positively
runneth over.

I PRAY YOU SLAY

be your most awesome
and authentic self –

for that is the way
of the slayer.

NO HIDING

please do not,
not even for a moment,
hide the boundless gloriousness
that is you.

we need your light in this world, friend.

KEEP SHINING

that light of yours is
mind-blowingly bright,
so please, please, please
keep shining.

SECRET WEAPON

you will not draw them in
with your cool.

nobody worth knowing is
interested in a facade
you've created
or a persona
you're trying on like
a glittery outfit.

your tribe will present itself
when you are your absolute
uncoolest –
when your crazy and kooky self
is dancing around
with arms waving wildly.

trust is built through
radical moments of authentic bliss.

never forget that your secret weapon
is always joy.

ZZZ

when in doubt,
nap it out.

CHOOSE THE LIGHT

the light is where joy likes to hang out.

you and some joy
could get a gang together
and really kick the shit out of
some fear and doubt.

WHAT THE SHIT?

ever have one of those days
that leaves you
scratching your head
and wondering
"what in the fuckity hell went wrong?"

yeah –
me neither.

SMALL-ISH

we all feel small sometimes.

but just because
we feel small,
doesn't mean
we have to act small.

PERFECT PAIR

you deserve
a break,
a moment,
a breath,
a sigh –

all of which pair perfectly
with a shot of tequila.

DO RIGHT

all you can do is
the next right thing
and then
the next right thing after that.

or at least as "right"
as you can manage.

oh, yes
and forgive yourself
as many times
as you need to.

then do the next,
next right thing.

OM IT OUT

take it easy,
my divine
little cupcake.

KEEP OFF

stake your claim
around your energy.

set your boundaries
and let them stand.

protect does not equal reject.

INSPIRED

we all have the ability
to inspire someone –
mostly through unabashed truth-telling
and
a double scoop of authenticity.

REMEMBER

remember the ooey-gooey,
chocolate-covered center of you,
the gorgeous part you'd risk it all
to rediscover?

give that part of you
a high-five
and then head out
and be awesome.

GRACE

use it or
lose it.

BEAUTIFUL MESS

things can get fuzzy
and out of focus,
which is not entirely
pleasant.

but you can choose
to embrace
the mess –
and call it
"beautiful."

YOU DO YOU

sing louder
than the radio.

dance with
or without
an ounce of rhythm.

tell jokes
even if you forget
the punchline.

wear that messy bun
like a goddamn tiara.

you do you –
so. freaking. hard.

BAD GUYS

it seems
like there is always
a bad guy.

a person determined
to cause pain
because they are hurt.

don't let it
be you.

don't let your pain,
your hurt,
or your scars
lead you to put on the black hat.

your spirit
was meant to ride
the white horse,
to rescue the weak and weary,
to give hope
and greet the end of the day
with love still in your heart.

you see,
bad guys never really win.

they just stay broken
and let their fear
look like power.

LUCKY YOU

as luck would have it,
luck has almost nothing
to do
with luck
at all.

you listened,
you learned,
you took a leap,
you fell,
you learned some more,
you dusted yourself off,
and you tried again.

and when you finally succeeded,
they called you lucky,
because it's too scary
to realize
just how powerful we really are.

THE THRILL

it doesn't always look
like you think
it will.

it doesn't always come
dressed in adrenaline
and leather boots.

most times
it's seeing something
old and familiar
in a new way.

most times
it gets your blood pumping
through simple surprise
and
a willingness
to open up
and see things
with new eyes.

CHOOSE

choose each
and every
thought
as if it were
perfectly-selected shoes
for a first date,
a comforter for your bed
that will bring you
the best night's sleep,
or
the name of a child
growing in your belly –

because your thoughts
determine your direction,
and your direction
determines your path,
and your path
determines your journey
and your journey
is why you are here.

choose wisely.

HARD THINGS

we are capable of
tackling the difficult
challenges in life.

but it's good to remember
that we don't always
have to.

if the challenge
doesn't serve your soul
or protect others,
sometimes it's okay
to give the hard thing
a hard pass.

EMILY HAINES LLOYD

THE AUDACITY

take your audacity
out for a spin
every now and then.

every once
in a while.

when you sense
the urge.

when you need it.

which is at least
every now and then
and more likely
every single day.

p.s.
practice makes perfect.

RESPONSIBILITY

used to be
responsibility
was a bummer,
because it meant
cleaning your room,
doing dishes,
and watching your mouth.

but

now that you're
older
and
wiser-ish,

you realize
you're responsible
for the joy
you exude,
the belonging
you create,
and
the peace
you feel.

gimme, gimme
all the
responsibilities.

GIVING

sometimes the most gracious
and bold move
you can make
does not require
any action
at all.

sometimes all you have to do
is be present
and create space
for someone
to sit in silence
with you.

even
(okay, especially)
yourself.

REPORT CARD

there is nothing to do
with the archaic notion
that we are being graded
on how we do life –

except take the
flimsy piece of paper
(real or imagined)
and tear it into
tiny pieces
and release it into the wind.

then pick up the pieces,
because while your soul
should never be judged,
nobody likes
a litter bug.

OLD STORIES

dear, sweet
soul –

do not weigh down
your spirit
with old stories
from your past.

each day
is a new page
on which to write
new stories
with different endings
and
a million
daring adventures
in between.

ABOUT THE AUTHOR

Emily Haines Lloyd is a freelance writer in Grand Rapids, Michigan. Emily has published inspirational posts on her Instagram and Facebook feeds as *Buddha-ish* – to remind others (not to mention herself) that the road to enlightenment ain't easy.

On weekends she can be found at art fairs and farmer's markets writing one-of-a-kind pep talk poems for anyone willing to step up to her table.

Emily also won a Charlie LeDuff essay contest in the *Detroit News* and was featured in the 2016 *Write Michigan* anthology.

Learn more at emilyhaineslloyd.com

Made in the USA
Middletown, DE
04 September 2019